Animal Habitats

The Dragonfly over the Water

Text by Christopher O'Toole

Photographs by Oxford Scientific Films

Gareth Stevens Publishing
Milwaukee

Contents

Note: The use of a capital letter for a dragonfly's name means it is a *species* of dragonfly (for example, Bluebell Dragonfly). The use of a lower case, or small, letter means that it is a member of a larger *group* of dragonflies. The species names of dragonflies in this book are their common, rather than scientific, names. This means that a dragonfly with a common name in one region may have a different name in another.

A quiet weedy pond makes an ideal breeding place for many kinds of dragonfly.

A Common Hawker Dragonfly perches on a waterside reed. Many species are brightly colored like this.

Dragonflies and where they live

Visit any weedy pond or slow, lazy river in summer, and you will eventually see some dragonflies. Over and near the water, these longbodied insects fly, some with long swoops, others with a rapid, darting flight. Many *species* are brightly colored, and all are a very important part of the waterside scene.

In their seemingly endless flight, the dragonflies are doing several things. Most will be feeding, for these acrobats of the air catch insect *prey* on the wing. Some will be males, patrolling up and down, looking for females to mate with. And others will be females, looking for places to lay their eggs, either in the water or in damp moss on waterside tree stumps.

Water is essential for dragonflies, for, as we shall see, these masters of the air have *larvae* which live under water. And, like the adults, the larvae are *predators*, catching and eating a wide variety of small, water-dwelling creatures.

There are about 5,000 different species of dragonflies in the world. They are found in many different kinds of *habitat*, but most live in warmer countries and usually close to water. However, dragonflies are fast and powerful fliers and often fly far from water. Indeed, some species have regular long-distance migrations, like birds.

In Europe and North America, many large species can be seen flying up and down forest tracks and clearings, far from water and looking for insect prey. They will even travel considerable distances into nearly waterless deserts. They have been seen in the deserts of Nevada, flying in the hundreds, over the heads of people, feeding on flies attracted to human sweat.

Dragonflies perch with their wings spread out.

The dragonfly's body

Flying with the dragonflies will be their more slender and delicate relatives, the damselflies. They, too, catch insect prey on the wing, they are often brightly colored, and they have larvae that live under water. But they differ from dragonflies in their slower, fluttering flight and their habit of flying slowly between dense waterside plants.

Another way to tell them apart is by the way they rest their wings. A perching dragonfly has its wings spread out flat, while a damselfly sits with its wings held vertically and lengthways over its body.

The bodies of dragonflies and damselflies are divided into the three body regions typical of insects: the head, *thorax*, and *abdomen*. The thorax has two pairs of wings. These are strengthened and kept rigid by a complex network of veins. Usually, the wings are clear and transparent, but many species have wings patterned with blotches of color. The thorax also has three pairs of legs. These are of very little use in walking, but are adapted for perching and grasping prey.

The long, thin abdomen consists of ten *segments* and contains the gut and the sex organs.

As in all insects, the outer skin, or cuticle, is made of a waterproof, translucent substance called chitin, which is both light and strong. The cuticle is also the insect's skeleton and all muscles are attached to it. Because it is on the outside of the body, enclosing the soft parts, it is called an external or *exoskeleton*. Insects breathe through pores in the cuticle called *spiracles*. Each spiracle connects with a dense network of breathing tubes called tracheae.

Damselflies perch with their wings folded over the body.

4

A waxy glow gives this dragonfly its beautiful blue color.

The most noticeable thing about the bodies of dragonflies and damselflies is their bright, attractive patterns. These give vivid flashes of color as the insects dart and flutter near stretches of water. The colors are produced in several ways. The pigments which make pale blues, greens, some reds, and some yellows are laid down in a layer of fat just under the cuticle. They fade very quickly after death, as the fat layer breaks down. Other colors, such as some reds and yellows and black, are permanent. They are actually laid down in the cuticle itself. Some colors may develop on the surface of the cuticle as a waxy glow, somewhat like the glow found on the skins of plums.

The most spectacular colors, though, are metallic blues, greens, brassy bronze, and rose. Metallic colors are not due to pigments, but are caused by microscopic structures in the cuticle. These structures break up and scatter light in such a way that metallic colors are reflected. A few species of dragonfly and damselfly have all these methods of producing colors, but most use only one or two ways.

The body plan of dragonflies has remained unchanged since the Carboniferous period (345-280 million years ago). Fossils about 280 million years old show there were giant species with wingspans of up to 2 ft 9 inches (75 cm). They flew through the hot, humid forests, the remains of which we know as coal. Modern species are much smaller, with wingspans ranging from about 1 inch to 7 inches (3 to 18 cm).

A close-up of a dragonfly's wing. A dense network of veins makes it rigid and strong.

The dragonfly's head

Anyone who has tried to get close to a resting dragonfly knows just how difficult this can be. One sudden movement, and the insect is gone. If, however, you can get close enough, you will see immediately why this happens. More than half of the total area of the large head is taken up by two huge eyes, giving the insect all-around vision. The head is also very mobile, and this, together with the massive eyes, enables dragonflies to be alert at all times.

The eyes are called *compound eyes* because each one is made up of thousands of tiny *facets*. Indeed, there may be up to 30,000 facets per eye. Each facet is a separate unit, with its own lens and nerve connection to the brain. Such eyes are very sensitive to movement. Most species can detect movement at distances up to 42 ft (13 m), but some large dragonflies have eyes which can perceive movements up to 65 ft (20m) away. Eyes like this are vital for the dragonfly's style of life. They help it escape enemies, detect prey, and find mates.

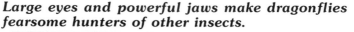

Large eyes and powerful jaws make dragonflies fearsome hunters of other insects.

Damselflies also have large eyes, but they are separated.

In dragonflies, the eyes occupy the top of the head as well as the sides. In many species, the eyes actually meet on the top of the head. In damselflies, the eyes are widely separated and fully cover the sides of the head.

On top of the head, between the eyes, there are three simple eyes, or *ocelli*. They are arranged in a triangle and, unlike the compound eyes, are not involved with seeing. Instead, they are very sensitive to changes in the brightness of daylight.

Between the eyes, there are two feelers, or *antennae*. They contain senses of touch and, possibly, hearing and smell. In comparison with the antennae of other insects, they are very small and have only five segments. This is what we might expect in insects like dragonflies, which rely so heavily on their excellent sight.

When the dragonfly is in flight the whole head acts as a balancing organ. It is attached to the thorax by a very narrow neck. When the position of the head changes relative to the rest of the body, this is recorded by special organs in the head. The insect then adjusts its position by wing movements.

The head also has a pair of powerful jaws. Each is armed with several teeth on its cutting edge, and together they crunch up insect prey into tiny pieces.

Open places like this clearing are ideal hunting grounds for dragonflies.

Hunting on the wing

Although dragonflies will feed close to water, most of their flying activity near ponds and rivers is concerned with mating and egg-laying. But when one sees dragonflies far from open water, say, hunting up and down forest paths, it means only one thing: feeding.

Dragonflies catch and eat insect prey, mainly flies, on the wing. And if we watch them carefully, we can see that there are two kinds of flying behavior. Large species patrol up and down, with regular upward swoops. Each swoop is an attack on a flying insect. These dragonflies are called "hawkers." Smaller dragonflies perch on something prominent, like a branch overhanging a track, and dart upwards now and then to catch a passing insect. They usually return time after time to the same perches. They are called "darter" dragonflies.

Think of a fly, hovering over a woodland path. Have you ever tried to catch one? It is difficult! Like dragonflies, they react to the slightest movement. But dragonflies can and do catch flies. Just how they do it is a fascinating story, and it all has to do with their wonderful eyes, amazing powers of flight, and special legs.

Hawker or darter, whatever their flight patterns, dragonflies tend to attack their prey from below. The facets on the upper half of each eye are large and sensitive to moving objects. The lower half of the eye has smaller facets and detects still objects below the dragonfly. It seems to be easier for a dragonfly to spot an insect silhouetted in the sky above than a non-moving one below it. However, dragonflies do pick insects off tree trunks and people, while one species, the Brown Hawker, sometimes catches small frogs off of the ground.

But to return to the fly. Having spotted it, the dragonfly must put out a tremendous burst of speed if it is to have any chance of catching such a fast-flying insect. Dragonflies can accelerate rapidly and have been recorded flying at speeds of 15-21 mph (25-35 kph). It has been calculated that one Australian species can fly at 35 mph (57 kph)!

In reaching the fly, the dragonfly may have to rely not only on speed, but also on agility. Indeed, dragonflies can fly backwards, loop the loop, and hover. And all of these skills stem from the way the thorax is built and the wings are powered.

Dragonflies can live even in deserts, where they breed in temporary pools. They may hunt many miles from the nearest water.

The thorax of dragonflies and damselflies is tilted backwards and upwards. It houses large and powerful flight muscles and gives the thorax a hunched-up appearance. The wing muscles are connected directly to the four wings and all wings can beat independently of one another. This is unique. In all other insects, the main flight muscles connect the upper and lower inner surfaces of the thorax, making the wings beat together in unison. Bees, for example, can beat 300 times per second, but dragonflies, with their more primitive system, can manage no more than 30 beats per second. Nevertheless, dragonflies are remarkable acrobats in the air.

The dragonfly has now reached the fly and uses its legs to grasp it. Just as the upper side of the thorax is skewed backward, so the underside is skewed forward. This means that the six legs jut forward in a grasping fashion. They are covered with spines and bristles and form a kind of basket which helps the dragonfly catch its prey.

The dragonfly uses its front legs to pass the prey to its mouthparts. The lower lip holds it, while the massive jaws cut it up into tiny pieces. All of this has taken less than one thousandth of the time it has taken you to read these paragraphs. Dragonflies are truly super-efficient aerial hunters.

A Common Darter Dragonfly perches as it waits for passing insect prey.

This Keeled Skimmer Dragonfly eats a moth it has caught on the wing.

Although damselflies are weaker fliers than dragonflies, they, too, catch insect prey on the wing, especially flies. They tend to hunt nearer to water than the dragonflies. They often feed on greenfly on plants and have been seen taking spiders from flowers.

Dragonflies often gather in large numbers where there is lots of prey. This is called "swarm feeding" and is often seen where mating swarms of midges dance over tree tops. In Africa, dragonflies often follow people and large animals walking through the bush. They feed on resting insects that have been disturbed from plants.

Beekeepers may sometimes find dragonflies a nuisance. The dragonflies hover near hives and catch the honeybees as they come out. But on the whole, dragonflies are useful insects because they kill large numbers of blood-sucking flies.

This Common Red Damselfly is eating a young Common Blue Damselfly it has caught.

A Four-spotted Chaser Dragonfly basks in the morning sun to raise its body temperature.

Temperature control: warming up and cooling down

Damselflies and dragonflies spend much of their time feeding and searching for mates, and for both these activities, they need to be able to fly. But, being insects, dragonflies are cold-blooded, at least when resting and inactive. In other words, when at rest and when the muscles are not making heat by working, the insect's body temperature drops until it is the same as the air around it. This means that each morning, after resting overnight, the dragonfly must warm up its flight muscles to the correct temperature before it can fly.

Dragonflies and damselflies spend the night perched on plants. In the morning, if a dragonfly is very chilled, it will begin by shivering its wing muscles rapidly. This produces heat and, in smaller species, flight is possible when the muscles warm up to 56-59° F (12-15° C). Large hawker dragonflies, however, need the muscles to be at 127° F (53° C).

Having warmed up enough to fly, the dragonfly can go about its daily business of feeding and finding mates or places to lay eggs. If the temperature drops, say in cloudy weather, dragonflies often settle on warm stones and absorb heat from them. If, however, the weather is hot and the insects have been very active, all the muscular activity may

Sometimes dragonflies absorb heat from warm objects, like this Emperor Dragonfly perching on a sun-warmed log.

cause overheating. So the dragonflies then have to find ways of cooling down.

There are four ways dragonflies can do this. The simplest is to fly to shade and perch there. But shade may be absent or hard to find, in which case darter dragonflies land and perch in a very strange way. They face away from the sun and point their abdomens directly at it, so that the smallest possible area of the body is exposed to the direct rays. At the same time, the wings shade the thorax. This is called the "obelisk position."

The larger hawkers do things differently. They remain in flight and divert hot blood from the thorax into the abdomen, where it is cooled before returning to the thorax. Here, the abdomen is acting like the radiator of a car.

Some hawkers also cool down by gliding for periods of up to 15 seconds while in mid-flight. The back wings are broader at their bases, which gives extra lift, making gliding possible. As the insect glides, the flight muscles stop producing heat and cool air flows over the thorax, lowering its temperature.

Cooling down: a dragonfly points its abdomen at the sun, reducing the area of its body exposed to heat and using its wings for shade.

This Common Darter male guards his territory from a prominent branch.

Courtship and territory

Courtship and mating in dragonflies is fascinating and easy to watch. Find a quiet spot on the banks of a pond or river and sit still. You will soon see the amazing story unfold.

The best time is around mid-day, in hot, sunny weather. This is when most females arrive on the scene. Males will have arrived earlier, having finished feeding away from the water. The males of some species seem to have no special courtship behavior. Instead, they use "rush-and-grab" tactics and will try to grasp any passing female, sometimes even males, and not always of the same species. A Broad-bodies Chaser Dragonfly male was once seen trying to mate with a hornet, which has orange markings similar to the female dragonfly.

Mistakes like this give us a clue as to why the males of many dragonfly and damselfly species have developed such special courtship behavior. A courting male goes through a little ritual which is unique to his species. This helps a female recognize him as a member of her own kind. It also probably allows her to tell whether a male is going to be suitable as a mate.

A male Ten-spot Chaser guards his territory over a pond. He uses his patterned wings in his courtship flight dances.

There are many kinds of courtship. The males of some species with patterned wings flutter in a special dancing flight in front of the female. Others dangle distinctly-patterned legs in front of the females and lure them into their *territory*. The males of some damselfly species carry out a little fluttering dance in front of a resting female. This makes the female go into a kind of trance.

The males of many species set up territories at ponds or along sections of rivers. A male patrols and inspects his territory constantly. He chases out rival males and tries to mate with any females which enter. The size of a territory depends on the size of the species concerned and the numbers of males competing for areas of their own. The largest and strongest males maintain the largest and best territories, and they mate more often than smaller and weaker males.

The male Banded Demoiselle, a beautiful, metallic green damselfly, has a special egg-laying territory within his main territory. Part of his courtship behavior involves leading the female to some water weeds to show her the place where she can later lay her eggs.

A male Splendid Damselfly (above) courts a female (below). His dancing flight has put her into a kind of trance.

A male Small Red Damselfly holds a female with his claspers in the "tandem" position.

Mating

Despite the wide range of courtship behavior in dragonflies and damselflies, they all mate in much the same way. Their mating behavior is rather unusual, however, because of the unusual way in which the males are built.

Like all other male insects the male dragon- or damselfly produces *sperm* inside his abdomen. And as with other insects, these sperm will eventually leave the male's body through an opening and fertilize the female's eggs. But here the similarity ends. Before a male dragon- or damselfly looks for a mate, he transfers the sperm away from the opening of the abdomen and back into another segment. There he stores the sperm inside his abdomen, in a special pouch.

With the sperm stored in this way, the male will now use the pair of *claspers* at the end of his abdomen to grasp a female. Male dragonflies grasp the back of the female's head, while a male damselfly grabs the front of the female's thorax. A pair may fly in this "tandem" position for a little while before settling on a stone or branch.

After a short tandem flight, a male and female of the Small Red Damselfly have settled and taken up the "wheel" position for mating.

Dragonflies mate in the "wheel" position, too, but the male holds his mate by her head rather than by her thorax.

The female now bends her abdomen so that the opening of her abdomen engages with the male's. The pair are now in the "wheel" position, and they may fly a little before landing again. When they finally come to rest, you may think that mating has finally started. But you would be wrong.

When they are in the wheel position, the male removes any sperm deposited in the female's body by previous males. He does this before depositing his own sperm to make sure that his sperm will be the first out of the female's abdomen when she later releases some to fertilize her eggs. By being the last male, an individual makes sure that it is his sperm, and not a rival's, which fertilized the eggs—so only he will be the father of the next generation.

A mating pair of the Blue-tailed Damselfly in the "wheel" position.

A Brown Hawker Dragonfly female lays eggs in the underwater stem of a plant.

Egg laying

The male's role does not end with mating. Egg laying usually follows soon afterward, and in many species, the male stays nearby. The pair may adopt the tandem position again before flying to an egg-laying spot. In some species, however, the male detaches himself from the female and follows her at a distance. In either case, he protects her from the attention of other males. This is not out of courtesy. Indeed, it is highly selfish behavior. Having removed the sperm of rivals from his mate it pays for him to stay with her to be sure that when she lays her eggs, no other male has a chance to mate with her beforehand. In other words, he is protecting his investment.

Dragonflies lay their eggs in water or in very damp places close to water. The Darter Dragonfly lays directly into the water, usually in tandem with a male. The pair skim over the water, bobbing up and down regularly so that the tip of the female's abdomen dips below the surface and releases eggs. Eggs laid in this way are usually round. Other species lay their eggs in plant tissues. In these cases, the eggs are usually long and sausage-shaped.

A Beautiful Damselfly female lays her eggs in the leaf of a water plant.

Held by her protective mate, a female damselfly lays her eggs in an old, water-logged stem.

Damselfly females are almost always attended by males when they lay eggs. The males remain attached in the tandem position, even when the female backs down under the water to insert eggs into the stem or leaf of a water plant. She may remain submerged for an hour. She may even drag the male down with her. If he becomes detached, he will remain fluttering in the air above her. The males of some species will try and rescue their mates if they are attacked from below by a fish or water spider.

Females have an egg-laying tube or *ovipositor* at the rear end of the body. The size and shape of this depends on where the species lays eggs. It is small in species which lay directly into water. Those that lay eggs into water plants have a curved, blade-like ovipositor, that cuts a little slit in the plant for the eggs.

Females of the Golden-ringed Dragonfly have a large, wedge-shaped ovipositor. This is perfect for laying in shallow mud or streams with gravel bottoms. She is unattended by her mate. Solo egg-laying is also found in the Southern Hawker. The females of this species lay eggs in damp moss or waterlogged tree stumps by the sides of ponds.

Sometimes, a female damselfly lays her eggs while completely underwater, her whole body covered by a silvery air bubble.

Eggs of the Broad-bodied Chaser Dragonfly that have settled on some water weed.

Growing up under water

The eggs of dragonflies and damselflies eventually hatch into larvae. The larvae (or nymphs) are drab and speckled. They creep about in the mud or among water weeds. Damselfly larvae are long and thin, and each has three leaf-like outgrowths at the end of the abdomen. These are gills and are richly supplied with air tubes, or tracheae. The tracheae radiate to all parts of the body, supplying it with oxygen. At the same time, the waste gas, carbon dioxide, is carried along the tracheae to the outside. The larvae of damselflies swim with a side-to-side motion, and the gills give added thrust, somewhat like the flippers of a seal.

Dragonfly larvae are squat and slightly flattened. They have no external gills. Instead, the tracheal gills are in an expanded chamber inside the abdomen, at the end of the gut. The larva can suck water into this and then squirt it out rapidly, enabling it to rush forward with a kind of jet propulsion.

A damselfly larva, with its three leaf-like gills.

The larva of a large hawker dragonfly molts its skin.

A larva of the Brown Hawker Dragonfly eats a small fish, having caught it with its remarkable "mask."

Unlike, say, beetles and butterflies, there is no pupa or chrysalis stage in the development of dragonflies and damselflies. Instead, the larva changes and grows in several stages until the adult insect is formed. There are 10-16 larval stages (or *instars*), each separated by a *molt*. After the fourth instar, wing buds develop and increase in size after every molt. The whole larva increases in size after each molt while the new skin is still soft. After the final molt, the adult dragonfly emerges.

The larval stage in some large dragonflies may last 2-5 years. Others, especially in hot countries, may complete their development in less than 100 days.

Like the adults, the larvae are eager predators. They eat a wide range of small creatures, including water fleas, worms, snails, the larvae of beetles, and other insects, tadpoles, and small fish. They are well-equipped, with eyes that are sensitive to the slightest movement and antennae that are able to detect vibrations in the water set up by prey.

The larvae seize prey in a unique and spectacular way. The lower lip (or labium) is a modified, hinged structure called a *mask*. At rest, this is folded under the head. But when prey is detected within reach, the mask shoots out and back in about 25 thousandths of a second. Prey is speared on two hooks at the end of the mask and brought back to the jaws to be eaten.

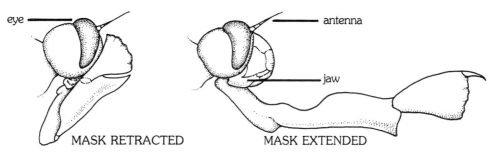

eye — antenna

jaw

MASK RETRACTED   MASK EXTENDED

The mask of the dragonfly larva.

A larva of the Broad-bodied Chaser Dragonfly climbs up a twig and out of the water.

Emergence

Shortly before they are ready to emerge as adults, dragonfly and damselfly larvae move to the edges of the pond or stream. They may remain in shallow water for a few days, searching for projecting logs, stems, or reeds on which to climb out. During this time, their eyes grow larger and the larvae stop feeding.

In warm countries, final emergence from the water takes place at night in order to avoid being eaten by birds. In cooler countries, the larvae leave the water either at dusk or just after dawn, though some species leave during the day. Many daytime emergers fall prey to birds.

The larval skin begins to split and the head of the new Broad-bodied Chaser Dragonfly appears.

After crawling up a stem or log, the larva wriggles its abdomen from side to side. This tests its grip and, possibly, checks the amount of room available for the later expansion of its wings. The larva then remains motionless for about 45 minutes, until a split in the cuticle appears between the wing buds. At this point, in damselflies, the head and thorax emerge from the split, and the insect moves forward to pull out its abdomen. In dragonflies, the head and thorax emerge completely and hang backwards for 10 to 20 minutes. Eventually, the new dragonfly makes rocking movements and pulls the rest of its body out. It now sits on the cast skin.

What happens next is the same for both dragonflies and damselflies. The crumpled forewings slowly expand as blood is pumped through the network of veins. Fluid between the upper and lower wing membranes is drained, and the wings begin to lose their milky appearance. The abdomen expands to its full size, and the insect's cuticle begins to harden and darken. But the full adult colors take several days to develop. During this early stage of adult life, the insects feed and improve their flying skills. Full development can take from a few days to up to two weeks in some species. The adults do not return to the water until they are ready to mate. Unlike the larva, an adult dragonfly will have just a few weeks of life—perhaps a month or so at the most.

Before removing the rest of its body, the young dragonfly hangs with its head downward for a few minutes.

The new Broad-bodied Chaser Dragonfly rests on its larval skin while its wings expand and harden and its colors develop.

This is the largest damselfly in the world. It lives in the forests of Central and South America, where it flies at night, stealing prey from spiders' webs.

Dragonflies around the world

With a total of 5,000 species in the world, it is not surprising that there are many dragonflies with unusual ways of life. One of the weirdest is a group of giant damselflies that live in the tropical forests of Central and South America. They are the largest living species, with wingspans of up to 7 inches (18 cm). The adults fly by night and steal the prey of spiders from their webs. They fly through the web with such force that they are not trapped by it.

The larvae of these giants develop in small, waterfilled holes in rotten and fallen logs. Other larvae live in unusual habitats, too. Some species live in the water which collects around the leaf bases in tropical plants called bromeliads. There are even a few species where the larvae have abandoned water altogether. They live in damp leaves on the floor of tropical forests. Perhaps the strangest larvae are those of an African Hawker Dragonfly. These larvae live in torrential waterfalls, even in the huge and famous Victoria Falls on the Zambesi River. They cling to the undersides of stones. The adults live and fly in the spray zone at the sides of waterfalls.

There are several dragonfly species that breed in the temporary pools in hot, dry parts of Africa. When the pools begin to dry up, the adults leave and migrate to areas where rain is about to fall. They do this by flying up very high until they are caught by strong, hot winds. When these hit currents of cool air, rain falls and new pools are formed.

In North America, there is a large hawker which migrates north from the US to Canada in early spring and breeds there. The new generation migrates south to avoid the winter. The greatest migrant, however, is a species known as the Globe-trotter. This hawker lives in warm countries in many parts of the world. It has been seen flying at 16,400 ft (5,000 m) in the Himalayan mountains, and a migratory cloud of Globe-trotters was once seen from a ship 290 miles (466 km) from land and 900 miles (1,448 km) from Australia, where it was thought the dragonflies had come from.

A South American damselfly larva in the water in the leaf base of a bromeliad plant. Here it eats mosquito larvae. There is room for only one damselfly larva.

A Keeled Skimmer Dragonfly is eaten by a spider after being trapped in the web.

Enemies

The eggs, larvae, and adults of dragonflies have a wide range of enemies both in and out of the water. There are several kinds of minute parasitic wasps whose larvae live inside and eat the eggs of dragonflies. The female wasps "fly" through the water, using their wings as paddles, as they search for dragonfly eggs to pierce with their ovipositors.

Although dragonfly larvae are fierce predators and large individuals will eat small fish, those same fish will eat larvae when the larvae are small. Indeed, dragonfly larvae are important food for pike and trout. They are also eaten by water spiders, water bugs, beetles, and newts. Certain kinds of duck eat them, and many are taken by herons.

Blackbirds are an unexpected enemy. They catch larvae from shallow waters by hovering over them and picking them out with their feet. Large dragonfly larvae will eat smaller ones, and cannibalism sometimes happens when there is overcrowding.

The larvae are not entirely defenseless, though. Many bottom-dwellers hide under mud and debris, and others have speckled markings that make them resemble their background. And some larvae are very spiny, making them difficult for fish to swallow.

Dragonflies are most helpless just after emergence from the water. For example, in southern England, up to 5 per cent may be eaten by birds such as blackbirds and sparrows. Some are eaten by large dragonflies, and in Africa, many emerging larvae are eaten by crocodiles.

Adult dragonflies rely on rapid, agile flight to avoid predators. But many are caught by swifts, herons, and ducks. Egg-laying females may be attacked by fish, while robber flies are also a danger to dragonflies flying in dry areas.

One of the most interesting enemies is a type of parasitic flatworm called a fluke. Part of its life is spent inside dragonflies, part inside birds. Larvae of the fluke fall into ponds with bird droppings. They get sucked into the rectal gill chamber of a dragonfly larva and burrow into the muscles, where they start to grow and eventually become adults. If the dragonfly is eaten by a bird, the flukes enter its body and the cycle starts all over again.

Being infected by flukes increases the chances of a dragonfly being eaten because the flukes cause an irritation that makes the insect fly up in the air. When large numbers of dragonflies are affected in this way, they attract feeding birds.

A Bluebell Dragonfly trapped by a sundew plant in a marsh. The plant digests the dragonfly with special juices.

Dragonflies and people

In Britain and Europe, dragonflies have always been regarded as mysterious, sinister, and even dangerous. This is shown by some of the names people have given them. In Norway, they are called eye-stingers, while in Britain, they have been called snake-doctors, horse-adders, and horse-stingers. Perhaps these last two names come from the observation that dragonflies sometimes dart abruptly at horses. When they do this, they are catching horseflies. In this way, they benefit the horse rather than harm it.

Despite these names, dragonflies are harmless to humans. At least their beauty seems to appeal to the peoples of Europe. Finland, Switzerland, Yugoslavia, and Albania have all recently shown colorful dragonflies on their postage stamps.

By draining this pond, people have robbed some dragonflies of a place to breed. The dark rim at the water's edge is a mass of dying tadpoles.

Three beautifully-colored dragonflies, painted in a free and naturalistic style by a Chinese Ming dynasty master of the 15th century, form part of a famous handscroll called Early Autumn.

In South America and Africa, people have a much more practical attitude about dragonflies: they eat them! Dragonflies are also eaten in Sumatra, Indonesia, where larvae are served with tadpoles and small fish in a curried soup. In Malaysia and on the island of Lombok, Indonesia, dragonflies are eaten fried in oil with onions, having been caught on long sticks covered with glue. Dragonflies are thought to have medicinal value in China and Japan, and some species of hawker are sold as a cure for fevers and sore throats.

The Kofan Indians of Colombia decorate their noses with the patterned wings of damselflies. They also regard the giant damsels, which fly at night, as the souls of the dead. This is an interesting belief because the Japanese believe that "Shoryo-tombo," the Dragonfly of the Dead, is responsible for carrying the spirits of their ancestors to an annual festival.

Dragonflies are much-loved in Japan. Thirty-two species have popular names, and the insects are symbols of playfulness. They are celebrated in many poems and illustrated in paintings and prints. Indeed, dragonflies are so popular that they are one of the Emperor's emblems, and one of the many names for Japan — "Akitsu-shimu" — means Dragonfly Island. In China, where dragonflies are not so popular as in Japan, they have nevertheless been the subjects for some of the finest paintings on silk.

Life around water

Dragonflies and damselflies, both as adults and larvae, prey on a wide range of small animals. Adult dragonflies, in turn, are eaten by many birds. They are also eaten by both city and farm cats. The larvae are an important food for fish, beetles, bugs, and certain kinds of duck. Dragonflies and damselflies are, therefore, at the center of a complicated web of relationships between animals. The links between animals are called food chains. The diagram below gives an outline of some of these food chains.

Food chain

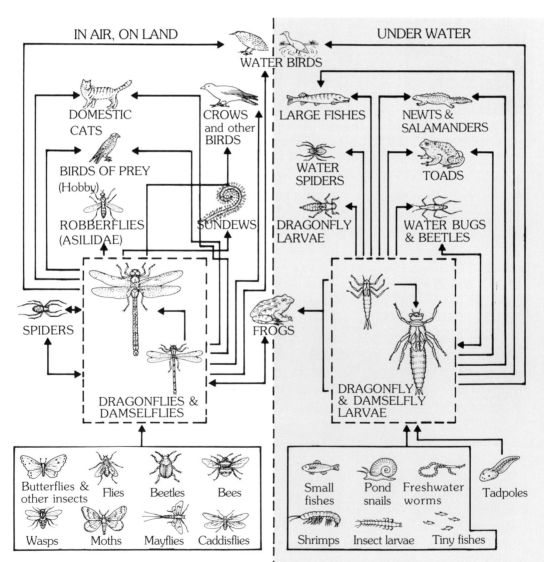

IN AIR, ON LAND

UNDER WATER

WATER BIRDS

DOMESTIC CATS

CROWS and other BIRDS

LARGE FISHES

NEWTS & SALAMANDERS

BIRDS OF PREY (Hobby)

WATER SPIDERS

TOADS

ROBBERFLIES (ASILIDAE)

SUNDEWS

DRAGONFLY LARVAE

WATER BUGS & BEETLES

SPIDERS

FROGS

DRAGONFLIES & DAMSELFLIES

DRAGONFLY & DAMSELFLY LARVAE

Butterflies & other insects   Flies   Beetles   Bees

Wasps   Moths   Mayflies   Caddisflies

Small fishes   Pond snails   Freshwater worms   Tadpoles

Shrimps   Insect larvae   Tiny fishes

Dragonflies, like this North American Brown-spotted Yellow-wing, need perching places around ponds and lakes.

Dragonflies require more than ponds, rivers, and food. The structure of the environment is important, too. Larvae need weeds or other projecting objects such as logs and tree stumps on which to climb out of the water when their development is complete. Adults need perching places such as waterside plants, trees, and bushes. But these are disappearing fast as modern farming methods demand the "cleaning up" of the countryside. Indeed, in Western Europe, despite an enormous surplus of grain, farmers are still paid to drain land and fill in ponds in order to grow wheat. Harmful chemicals used in farming, along with industrial waste, are poisoning our rivers.

It would be a tragedy if the beautiful dragons and damsels of the air were allowed to dwindle further or even disappear completely from the countryside. People can do much to help them survive by making ponds in fields, parks, and other types of land. Dragonflies and damselflies have one thing in their favor — they quickly colonize newly created habitats. If we are careful, the children of future generations might still be able to enjoy these fascinating insects as they dart and hover over the water.

Glossary and Index

These new words about dragonflies appear in the text on the pages shown after each definition. Each new word first appears in the text in *italics*, just as it appears here.

abdomen ......the rear of the three body parts of an insect, containing the gut and sex organs. **4, 13, 16, 17, 20, 23**

antennae ......feelers on the head that contain the sense of touch and, possibly, hearing and smell. **7, 21**

claspers ....a pair of hinged, finger-like structures at the end of a male dragonfly's abdomen that are used to grasp the female. **16**

compound eye ....an eye made up of thousands of facets, each with its own lens and connection to the brain. **6, 7**

exoskeleton ...the horny, outer shell of insects, which encloses and protects the soft parts and to which the muscles are attached. **4**

facet ....one of the thousands of units that make up a compound eye. **6, 9**

habitat ....the natural home of any animal or plant. **3, 25**

instar ....a stage between molts in an insect larva. **21**

larva ....(plural larvae) the form of an insect that emerges from the egg. **3, 4, 20, 21, 22, 23, 25, 26, 27, 30, 31**

mask ....the hinged lower lip used to catch prey and found only in the larvae of dragonflies and damselflies. **21**

molt ....to cast off an old skin or shell. **20, 21**

oscelli ....simple eyes, found in insects, with a single, thick lens - detect changes in the brightness of daylight. **7**

predator ....an animal that kills and eats other animals. **3, 26, 27**

prey ....an animal that is hunted and killed by another animal for food. **3, 4, 6, 7, 8, 9, 10, 11, 21, 22, 24, 30**

segment ....one of several similar parts forming the body or part of the body of an insect. **4, 16**

species ....a type of animal (or plant) that can interbreed successfully with others of its kind, but not with those of a different type. **3, 5, 6, 7, 8, 9, 12, 14, 15, 18, 19, 22, 23, 24, 25, 29**

sperm ....(short for spermatozoa): male sex cells that fertilize the eggs of the female. **16, 17, 18**

spiracles ....breathing holes in insects, each connecting with a fine network of tubes or tracheae, taking oxygen to all parts of the body. **4**

territory ....an area defended by a male for mating or feeding purposes. **14, 15**

thorax ....the middle of the three body parts of an insect, containing the flight muscles and bearing the wings and six legs. **4, 7, 9, 10, 13, 16, 17, 23**

Reading level analysis: SPACHE 3.8, FRY 6, FLESCH 74 (fairly easy), RAYGOR 6-7, FOG 7, SMOG 7.4

Library of Congress Cataloging-in-Publication Data   O'Toole, Christopher. The dragonfly over the water. (Animal habitats) Summary: Text and photographs depict dragonflies feeding, breeding, and defending themselves in their natural habitats. 1. Dragonflies—Juvenile literature. [1. Dragonflies] I. Oxford Scientific Films. II. Title. III. Series.   QL502.086   1988   595.7'33   87-42613   ISBN 1-55532-331-6   ISBN 1-55532-306-5 (lib. bdg.)

North American edition first published in 1988 by Gareth Stevens, Inc., 7317 West Green Tree Road, Milwaukee, WI 53223, USA
Text copyright © 1988 by Oxford Scientific Films. Printed in the United States of America.
All rights reserved. No part of this book may be reproduced in any form or by any means without permission in writing from Gareth Stevens, Inc.
Conceived, designed, and produced by Belitha Press Ltd., London.
Series Editor: Jennifer Coldrey. US Editor: Mark J. Sachner. Art Director: Treld Bicknell. Design: Naomi Games.
Line Drawings: Lorna Turpin. Scientific Consultant: Gwynne Vevers.

The publishers wish to thank the following for permission to reproduce copyright material: **Oxford Scientific Films Ltd.** for title page, pp. 5 below, 7, 14 above, 15, 17 above, 19 both, 20 all, 22 both, 23 both, 25, and back cover (G. I. Bernard); p. 2 (Gerald Thompson); pp. 3 and 18 above (Bob Frederick); pp. 4 above, 10, 12 above, 13, 16 below, and 17 below (Alastair Shay); p. 4 below (Peter Gathercole); front cover, pp. 5 above, 16 above, 18 below, and 26 (Tom Leach); p. 6 (Nick Woods); p. 9 (Sean Morris); p. 11 above (M. F. Black); p. 12 below (D. J. Stradling); pp. 14 below and 27 (Patti Murray/Animals Animals); p. 21 (Stephen Dalton); p. 24 (J. A. L. Cooke); p. 28 (David and Sue Cayless); p. 31 (E. R. Degginger); Prema Photos for p. 11 above (K. G. Preston). P. 29 is © 1987 The Detroit Institute of Fine Arts, Founders Society Purchase, General Membership and Donations Fund.